In loving memory of

Vernon Kroening (1948–1980)

and

Alan Steichen (1946–1979)

FOREWORD

At the Eucharistic celebration of the Detroit convention of the National Association of Pastoral Musicians in April, 1981, more than three thousand people sang out the ringing "We praise you, God" (No. 39 in this book) in the MONTANA tune arrangement of Henry Bryan Hays, O.S.B. (originally published by The Liturgical Press in *A Benedictine Book of Song*). This was that significant group's first appreciation of the art and talent of this Benedictine monk of Collegeville. Here it is my distinct privilege to introduce his first complete collection of hymns and songs.

For quite a few years now, Father Hays has been writing hymn tunes and songs, many of which have an inescapable Appalachian flavor (a conscious tribute to his Southern Protestant background). Some of these melodies are arranged in carefully wrought four-part harmony; others are intended solely for unison singing. The lyrics are gleaned from traditional sources; a few are original. Thus one has untouched poetry from several ages linked to a rich thesaurus of American traditional-style song. His beautiful setting of the WHITE MOUNTAIN tune (No. 3) most becomes the old Catholic favorite "Come, Holy Ghost." Another rugged melody perfectly fits Cardinal Newman's immortal *Credo*, "Firmly I believe and truly" (No. 11). Cross-relations in modal fashion and clear-ringing dissonances are carefully applied, such as in the WILD SEA song "Fierce was the wild billow" (No. 10) in the vivid translation by J. M. Neale from the ancient Greek hymn.

Hays's special affinity, I think, is to the metaphysical poets, particularly the religious genius of seventeenth-century England, George Herbert. The lilt of "Come, my way, my truth, my life" (No. 5) actually rivals the earlier twentieth-century version of Ralph Vaughan Williams. William Blake is similarly honored with Hays's superb EVELINGTON HEIGHTS version (No. 38). If some object that at times the language is antique, none can object to classics of the language being revivified with authentic American melodism.

Surely many parishes, choristers, and congregations will find this *Swayed Pines Song Book* a valuable companion to other hymnals or missalettes. All those interested in current hymn composition will want to study this important work of a relatively unknown but tried and true monastic voice. There is an interior purity to the sounds, the words themselves, that elevates the Christian imagination to prayer. There is on every page of this song book moving experience and profound sentiments that are religious at root. Yet the art remains clear and easy, the lines always singing themselves naturally.

Thus Hays has met a crying need. He has linked the finest English verse to colorfully harmonized American folk-style melody. My wish is that the book may be as popular as it seems successful in its aim. There is yet another link within it: Catholic mysticism and liturgical song. In this day and age in Church music that is a rare and worthy combination. These songs match the liturgical cycle and people's need to know the old and the new. And it's time more people know the work and genius of Henry Bryan Hays. He has hit upon something "earnest, earthless, equal, attuneable,/ vaulty, voluminous . . . stupendous" (Gerard Manley Hopkins, "Spelt from Sybil's Leaves").

Edward J. McKenna

Chicago, Illinois
April 29, 1981

TITLE INDEX

1. AS THE SUN WITH LONGER JOURNEY

2. COME, GRACIOUS SPIRIT

3. COME, HOLY GHOST

4. COME, HOLY GHOST, WITH GOD THE SON

5. COME, MY WAY, MY TRUTH, MY LIFE

6. CREATOR OF THE STARS AT NIGHT

7. EARTH'S MIGHTY MAKER WHOSE COMMAND

8. ETERNAL GLORY OF THE SKY

9. FAIREST LORD JESUS

10. FIERCE WAS THE WILD BILLOW

11. FIRMLY I BELIEVE AND TRULY

12. FLOWER OF WISDOM

13. FOREVER AND ALWAYS HE TRULY IS GOD

14. GOD MOVES IN A MYSTERIOUS WAY

15. GOD UNSEEN IS SEEN IN CHRIST

16. I LIFT MINE EYES UNTO THE HILLS

17. JESU, THOU JOY OF LOVING HEARTS

18. LET US, WITH A GLADSOME MIND

19. LORD, TEACH US HOW TO PRAY ARIGHT

20. LOVING SHEPHERD OF THY SHEEP

21. O BLEST CREATOR OF THE LIGHT

22. O CHRIST, WHO ART THE LIGHT AND DAY

23. O FOR A CLOSER WALK WITH GOD

24. O FOR A HEART TO PRAISE MY GOD

25. O GOD, CREATION'S SECRET FORCE

26. O LORD, MY PORTION AND MY CUP

27. O LOVE, HOW DEEP

28. O WOULD I WERE A SNOW WHITE DOVE

29. ONE THERE IS ABOVE ALL OTHERS

30. OUR LORD IS GOD WHO LIVES

31. PRAISE THE LORD OF HEAVEN

32. THE GOD OF LOVE MY SHEPHERD IS

33. THE KING OF LOVE MY SHEPHERD IS

34A. THE LORD'S MY SHEPHERD

34B. THE LORD'S MY SHEPHERD

35. THE LORD'S MY SHEPHERD

36. THE SONG OF THE TREES

37. THOSE WHO TRUST IN THEMSELVES

38. TO MERCY, PITY, PEACE AND LOVE

39. WE PRAISE YOU, GOD

40. WHEN I SURVEY THE WONDROUS CROSS

INDEX OF TUNE TITLES—

ANTIETAM	No. 33	GLORY BAND	No. 12	PEA RIDGE	No. 20
CHICKAHOMINY	No. 25	GLORY SKY	No. 8	PLUM RUN BEND	No. 30
CONRAD'S STORE	No. 40	HAMPTON STATION	No. 27	RADIANT LIGHT	No. 21
CORINTH	No. 2	HANOVER JUNCTION	No. 31	RAPPHANNOCK	No. 14
CREDO	No. 11	HARPERS FERRY	No. 17	ROSSVIEW	No. 16
CUMBERLAND GAP	Nos. 34A and 34B	HOPEWELL GAP	No. 18	SAYLOR'S CREEK	No. 36
DESERT SHRUB	No. 37	INDIAN MOUND	No. 15	SHILOH	No. 22
DUNKER CHURCH	No. 24	MANASSAS	No. 23	SOLID LAND	No. 7
ELKHORN TAVERN	No. 19	MECHANICSVILLE	No. 28	SUN JOURNEY	No. 1
EVELINGTON HEIGHTS	No. 38	MONOCACY	No. 5	SUNSHINE CHURCH	No. 35
FORT DONELSON	No. 13	MONTANA	No. 39	WHITE CHAPEL	No. 4
FRIEND JESUS	No. 29	MUNSON'S HILL	No. 9	WHITE MOUNTAIN	No. 3
GLORIETA PASS	No. 32	NEW HOPE CHURCH	No. 26	WILD SEA	No. 10
		NIGHT LIGHT	No. 6		

METRICAL INDEX

11.9. 11.7
FORT DONELSON (No. 13)

9.7 8.6. with Refrain
SAYLOR'S CREEK (No. 36)

8.8. 8.8.
CORINTH (No. 2)
WHITE CHAPEL (No. 4)
NIGHT LIGHT (No. 6)
SOLID LAND (No. 7)
CHICKAHOMINY (No. 25)

8.8.8. 7.8.
MONTANA (No. 39)

8.8.8.8.D
GLORY SKY (No. 8)
RADIANT LIGHT (No. 21)

8.7. 8.7. 8.7.
SUN JOURNEY (No. 1)

8.7. 8.7. 7.7.
FRIEND JESUS (No. 29)

8.7. 8.7.
CREDO (No. 11)
ANTIETAM (No. 33)

8.7. 8.7.D
MECHANICSVILLE (No. 28)

8.6. 8.6. 8.6.
NEW HOPE CHURCH (No. 26)

8.6 8.6.D
ELKHORN TAVERN (No. 19)

7.8. 7.8.
INDIAN MOUND (No. 15)

7.7. 7.7. 7.7. 7.7.D
HOPEWELL GAP (No. 18)

7.7. 7.7.
MONOCACY (No. 5)

7.7. 7.7.D
PEA RIDGE (No. 20)

6.9. 6.7. 7.8.
DESERT SHRUB (No. 37)

6.8. 7.7. 6.6.
PLUM RUN BEND (No. 30)

6.5. 6.5.D
HANOVER JUNCTION (No. 31)

6.4. 6.4.D
WILD SEA (No. 10)

5.5.7. 5.5.8.D
MUNSON'S HILL (No. 9)

5.4. 5.4.D
SUNSHINE CHURCH (No. 35)

C.M.
ROSSVIEW (No. 16)
CUMBERLAND GAP (Nos. 34A, 34B)

C.M.D.
RAPPAHANNOCK (No. 14)
MANASSAS (No. 23)
DUNKER CHURCH (No. 24)
GLORIETA PASS (No. 32)
EVELINGTON HEIGHTS (No. 38)

L.M.
WHITE MOUNTAIN (No. 3)
HAMPTON STATION (No. 27)
CONRAD'S STORE (No. 40)

L.M.D.
HARPER'S FERRY (No. 17)
SHILOH (No. 22)

IRREG.
GLORY BAND (No. 12)

INDEX OF AUTHORS

Saint Ambrose	No. 25
Anatolius	No. 10
William Henry Baker	No. 33
St. Bernard of Clairvaux	No. 17
William Blake	No. 38
Bro. Louis Blenkner, OSB	Nos. 13, 15, 30 37, 39
Simon Browne	No. 2
Thomas Brierly Browne	No. 31
William Cowper	Nos. 14, 23
John Patrick Earls	No. 1
Henry Bryan Hays	Nos. 16, 26, 28, 35, 36
George Herbert	Nos. 5, 32
Jane E. Lesson	No. 20
Benedict Neale Lundgren, OSB	No. 12
Rabanus Maurus	No. 3
John Milton	No. 18
J. Montgomery	No. 19
J. Henry Newman	No. 11
John Newton	No. 29
Isaac Watts	No. 40
Charles Wesley	No. 24

INTRODUCTION

To avoid any misunderstanding, let me confirm right away that the tunes in this collection are all mine. I have not used any pre-existing folk melodies, although some of the tunes have a folkish quality. Some of the confusion concerning my authorship of these melodies may arise from the fact that I have given each tune a name. I did this so that one can put a handle on a tune if another text is used. Several of my melodies in this book were originally written to different texts.

If I have used mainly old established texts, it is because I rather like them, and because it is so difficult to find poets who can or will write new ones that have any literary value. The popular so-called "relevant" texts used in the current guitar liturgy are not particularly my cup of tea.

All the hymns in this volume can be sung by an alert congregation, provided a leader with a good strong voice leads them. The four-part hymns also sound good sung a cappella by the choir. When sung by a mixed chorus, they should be transposed up; otherwise the alto and bass parts run too low. They were all, with one or two exceptions, conceived as higher anyway; they sound brighter and more alive that way.

And above all, they should not be taken too slowly. A dragged hymn is nothing but the abominable sin of sloth, a capital offense against the true meaning of the word *enthusiasm*.

Henry Bryan Hays, OSB

St. John's Abbey
Collegeville, Minnesota
May 14, 1981

1 AS THE SUN WITH LONGER JOURNEY

John Patrick Earls, OSB, b. 1935

Henry Bryan Hays
SUN JOURNEY 8.7. 8.7. 8.7

Moderate, yet sustained ♩=60

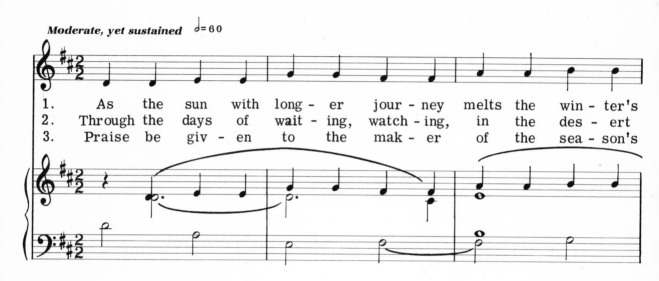

1. As the sun with long-er jour-ney melts the win-ter's
2. Through the days of wait-ing, watch-ing, in the des-ert
3. Praise be giv-en to the mak-er of the sea-son's

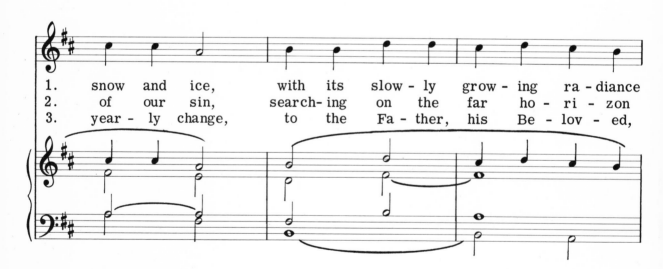

1. snow and ice, with its slow-ly grow-ing ra-diance
2. of our sin, search-ing on the far ho-ri-zon
3. year-ly change, to the Fa-ther, his Be-lov-ed,

1. warms the seed be - neath the earth, may the sun of
2. for a sign of cloud or wind, we a - wait the
3. in their liv - ing u - ni - ty, as the ev - er

1. Christ's up - ris - ing gen - tly bring our hearts to life.
2. heal - ing wa - ters of our Sav - ior's vic - to - ry.
3. turn - ing a - ges roll to their e - ter - nal rest.

2   COME, GRACIOUS SPIRIT

Simon Browne, 1680–1732

Henry Bryan Hays
CORINTH 8.8. 8.8.

Quietly flowing   ♩ = 52

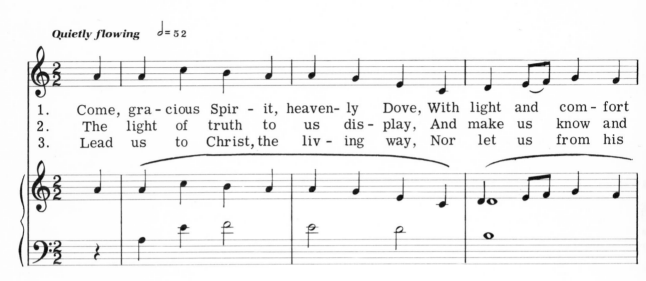

1. Come, gra-cious Spir - it, heaven- ly Dove, With light and com - fort
2. The light of truth to us dis - play, And make us know and
3. Lead us to Christ, the liv - ing way, Nor let us from his

1. from a bove; Be thou our guard- ian, thou our guide, O'er
2. choose thy way; Plant ho - ly fear in ev - ery heart, That
3. pas - tures stray; Lead us to ho - li - ness, the road That

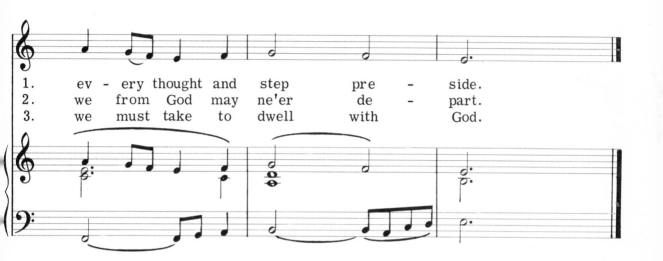

1. ev - ery thought and step pre - side.
2. we from God may ne'er de - part.
3. we must take to dwell with God.

4. Lead us to heaven, that we may share
   Fullness of joy for ever there;
   Lead us to God our final rest,
   To be with him for ever blest.

3 COME, HOLY GHOST

Veni Creator Spiritus
Rabanus Maurus, 776–656
Tr. Edward Caswall, 1814–78, alt.

Henry Bryan Hays
WHITE MOUNTAIN L.M.

Gently flowing ♩.= 48

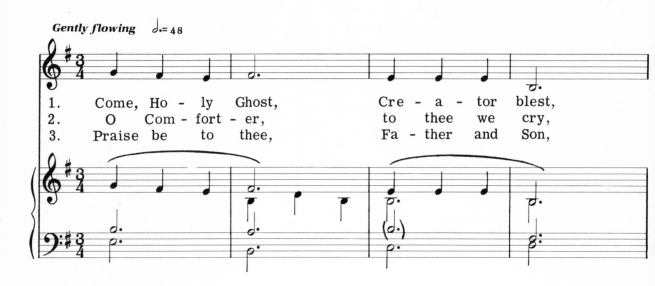

1. Come, Ho - ly Ghost, Cre - a - tor blest,
2. O Com - fort - er, to thee we cry,
3. Praise be to thee, Fa - ther and Son,

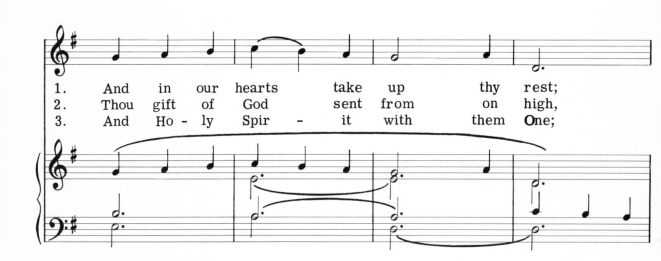

1. And in our hearts take up thy rest;
2. Thou gift of God sent from on high,
3. And Ho - ly Spir - it with them One;

4

COME, HOLY GHOST, WITH GOD THE SON

(Nunc, Sancte, nobis, Spiritus)

Ascribed to Saint Ambrose 340–97
Tr. J. M. Neale

Henry Bryan Hays
WHITE CHAPEL 8. 8. 8. 8.

With movement

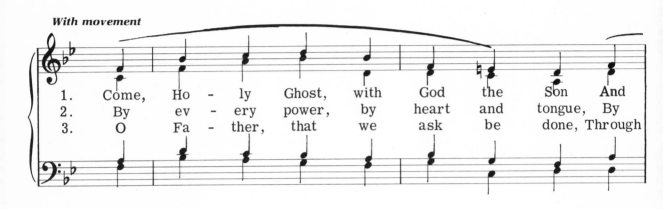

1. Come, Ho - ly Ghost, with God the Son And
2. By ev - ery power, by heart and tongue, By
3. O Fa - ther, that we ask be done, Through

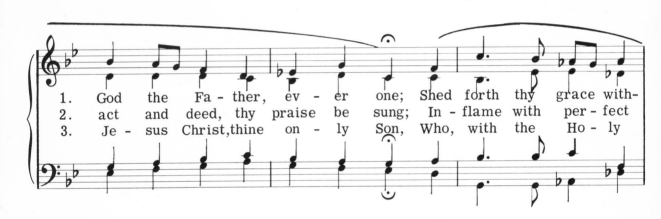

1. God the Fa - ther, ev - er one; Shed forth thy grace with-
2. act and deed, thy praise be sung; In - flame with per - fect
3. Je - sus Christ, thine on - ly Son, Who, with the Ho - ly

1. in our breast, And dwell with us a rea - dy guest.
2. love each sense, That oth - ers' souls may kin - dle thence.
3. Ghost and thee, Shall live and reign e - ter - nal - ly.

COME, MY WAY, MY TRUTH, MY LIFE

5

George Herbert, 1593–1632

Henry Bryan Hays
MONOCACY 7.7. 7.7.

Lilting (1 beat per measure)

1. Come, my Way, my Truth, my Life,
3. Come, my Joy, my Love, my Heart,

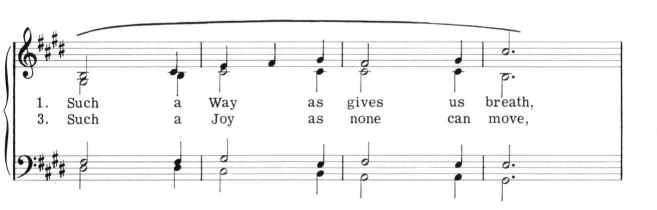

1. Such a Way as gives us breath,
3. Such a Joy as none can move,

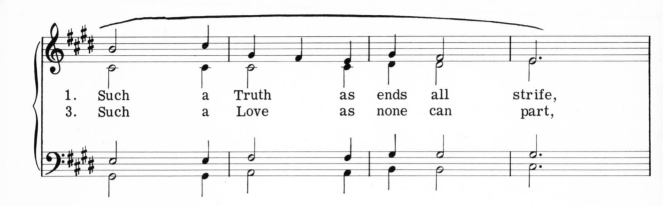

1. Such a Truth as ends all strife,
3. Such a Love as none can part,

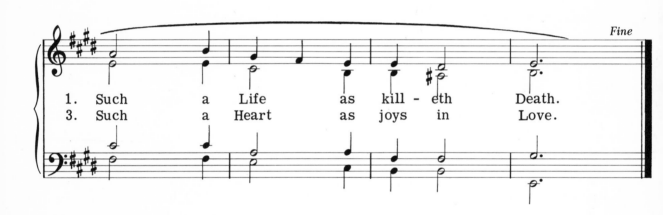

Fine

1. Such a Life as kill - eth Death.
3. Such a Heart as joys in Love.

2. Come, my Light, my Feast, my Strength,

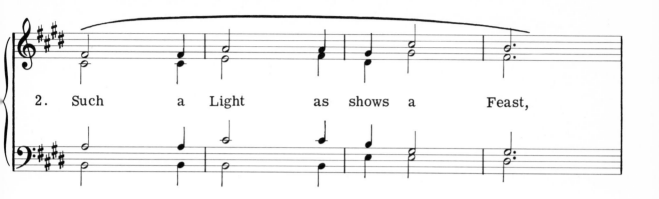

2. Such   a Light   as shows a   Feast,

2. Such   a Feast   as mends in   length,

Da capo al segno 𝄌

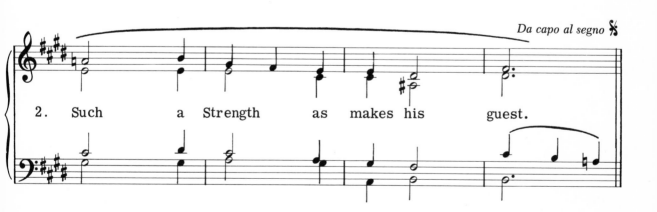

2. Such   a Strength   as makes his   guest.

6 CREATOR OF THE STARS AT NIGHT

(Conditor alme siderum)

7th cent.
Tr. J. M. Neale

Henry Bryan Hays
NIGHT LIGHT 8. 8. 8. 8.

Quiet & moving ♩ = 66

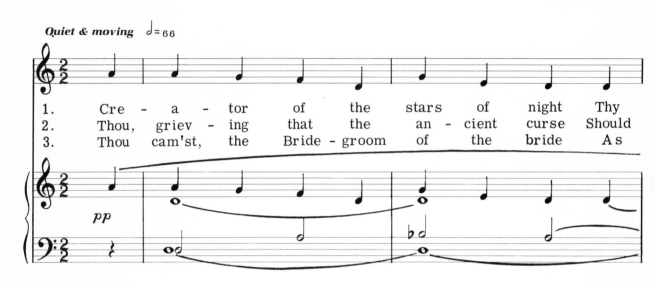

1. Cre - a - tor of the stars of night Thy
2. Thou, griev - ing that the an - cient curse Should
3. Thou cam'st, the Bride - groom of the bride As

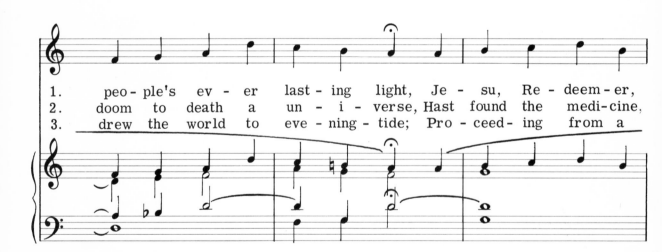

1. peo - ple's ev - er last - ing light, Je - su, Re - deem - er,
2. doom to death a un - i - verse, Hast found the medi - cine,
3. drew the world to eve - ning - tide; Pro - ceed - ing from a

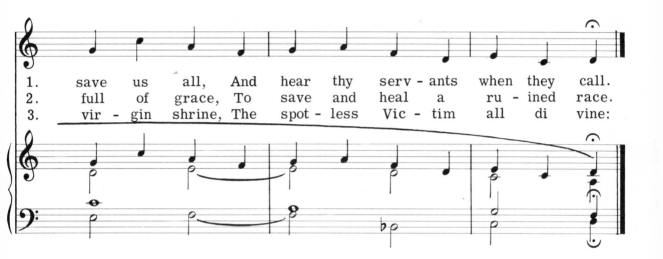

1. save us all, And hear thy serv - ants when they call.
2. full of grace, To save and heal a ru - ined race.
3. vir - gin shrine, The spot - less Vic - tim all di vine:

4. At whose dread name, majestic now,
   All knees must bend, all hearts must bow;
   And things celestial thee shall own,
   And things terrestrial, Lord alone.

5. O thou whose coming is with dread
   To judge and doom the quick and dead,
   Preserve us, while we dwell below,
   From every insult of the foe.

6. To God the Father, God the Son,
   And God the Spirit, Three in One,
   Laud, honour, might, and glory be
   From age to age eternally.

7 EARTH'S MIGHTY MAKER WHOSE COMMAND

(Telluris ingens Conditor)

c. 7th cent.
Tr. Anon. (1854)

Henry Bryan Hays
SOLID LAND 8. 8. 8. 8.

With spirit

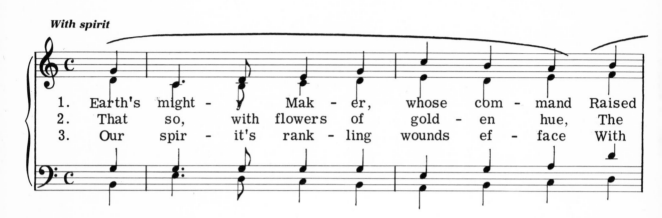

1. Earth's might-y Mak-er, whose com-mand Raised
2. That so, with flowers of gold-en hue, The
3. Our spir-it's rank-ling wounds ef-face With

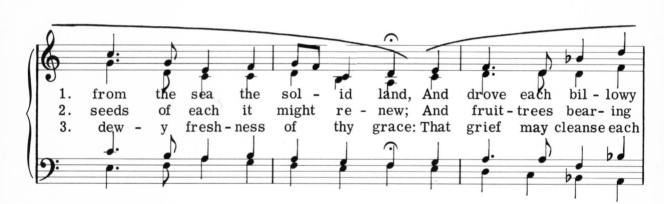

1. from the sea the sol-id land, And drove each bil-lowy
2. seeds of each it might re-new; And fruit-trees bear-ing
3. dew-y fresh-ness of thy grace: That grief may cleanse each

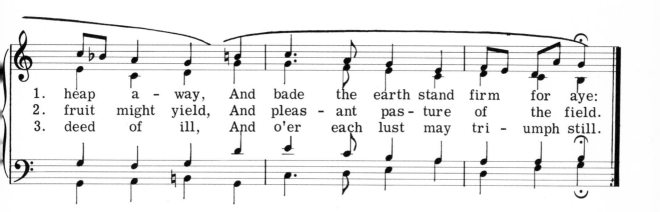

1. heap a - way, And bade the earth stand firm for aye:
2. fruit might yield, And pleas - ant pas - ture of the field.
3. deed of ill, And o'er each lust may tri - umph still.

4. Let every soul thy law obey,
   And keep from every evil way;
   Rejoice each promised good to win
   And flee from every mortal sin.

5. O Father, that we ask be done
   Through Jesus Christ, thine only Son,
   Who, with the Holy Ghost and thee,
   Doth live and reign eternally.

8 ETERNAL GLORY OF THE SKY

6th cent.
Tr. J. M. Neale

Henry Bryan Hays
GLORY SKY 8. 8. 8. 8. D

Brightly

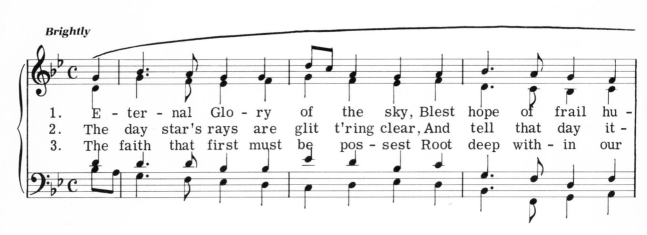

1. E - ter - nal Glo - ry of the sky, Blest hope of frail hu -
2. The day star's rays are glit t'ring clear, And tell that day it -
3. The faith that first must be pos - sest Root deep with - in our

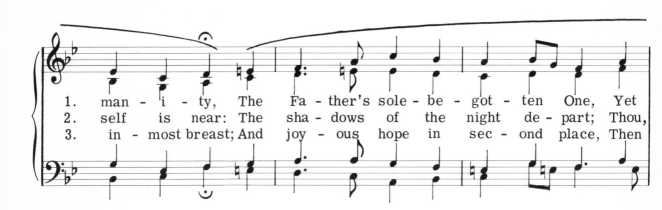

1. man - i - ty, The Fa - ther's sole - be - got - ten One, Yet
2. self is near: The sha - dows of the night de - part; Thou,
3. in - most breast; And joy - ous hope in sec - ond place, Then

1. born a spot - less Vir - gin's Son! Up - lift us with thine
2. ho - ly Light, il - lume the heart! With - in our sens - es
3. char - i - ty, thy great - est grace. All laud to God the

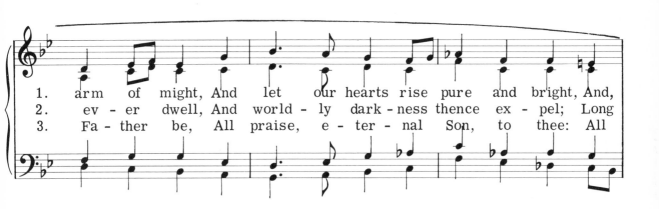

1. arm of might, And let our hearts rise pure and bright, And,
2. ev - er dwell, And world - ly dark - ness thence ex - pel; Long
3. Fa - ther be, All praise, e - ter - nal Son, to thee: All

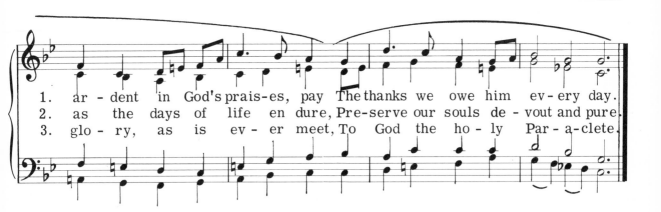

1. ar - dent in God's prais - es, pay The thanks we owe him ev - ery day.
2. as the days of life en dure, Pre - serve our souls de - vout and pure.
3. glo - ry, as is ev - er meet, To God the ho - ly Par - a - clete.

9

FAIREST LORD JESUS

Schönster Herr Jesu
Münster Gesangbuch, 1677
Schlesische Volkslieder, 1842
Tr. Joseph Augustus Seiss, 1823–1904, alt.

Henry Bryan Hays
MUNSON'S HILL 5.5.7. 5.5.8. D.

Slow waltz tempo ♩ = 112

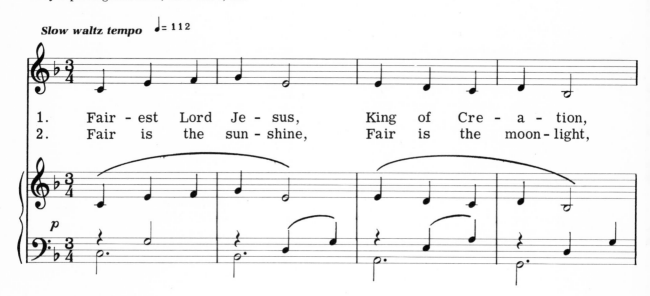

1. Fair - est Lord Je - sus, King of Cre - a - tion,
2. Fair is the sun - shine, Fair is the moon - light,

1. Son of God and Son of Man!
2. Bright the spark - ling stars on high;

1. Tru - ly I'd love thee, Tru - ly I'd serve thee,
2. Je - sus shines bright - er, Je - sus shines pur - er,

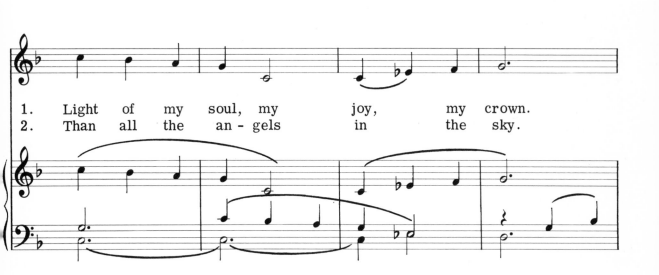

1. Light of my soul, my joy, my crown.
2. Than all the an - gels in the sky.

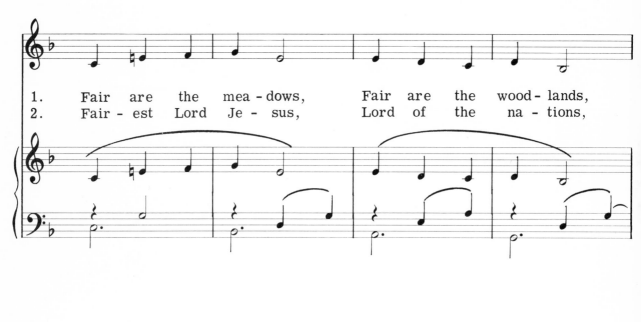

1. Fair are the mea-dows, Fair are the wood-lands,
2. Fair - est Lord Je - sus, Lord of the na - tions,

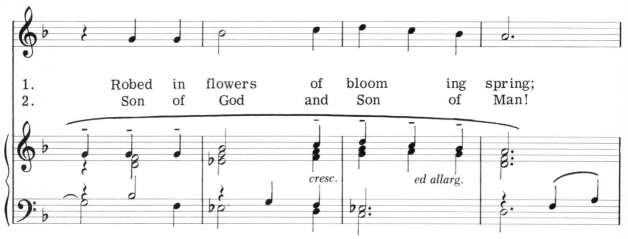

1. Robed in flowers of bloom ing spring;
2. Son of God and Son of Man!

cresc.

ed allarg.

1. Je - sus is fair - er, Je - sus is pur - er,
2. Glo - ry and hon - or, praise, a - do - ra - tion,

1. He makes our sor - rowing spir - it sing.
2. Now and for - ev - er - more be thine!

pp

10   FIERCE WAS THE WILD BILLOW

Greek hymn
Anatolius, 8th cent.
Tr. J. M. Neale

Henry Bryan Hays
WILD SEA 6.4. 6.4. D.

With energy

1. Fierce was the wild bil-low, Dark was the night;
2. Ridge of the moun-tain-wave, Low-er thy crest!
3. Je - su, De - liv-er - er, Near to us be;

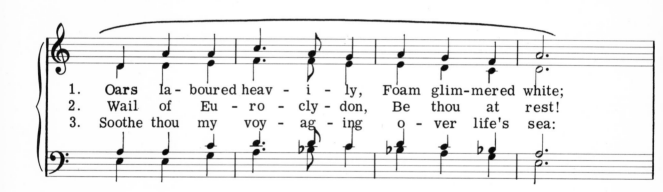

1. Oars la - boured heav - i - ly, Foam glim-mered white;
2. Wail of Eu - ro - cly - don, Be thou at rest!
3. Soothe thou my voy - ag - ing o - ver life's sea:

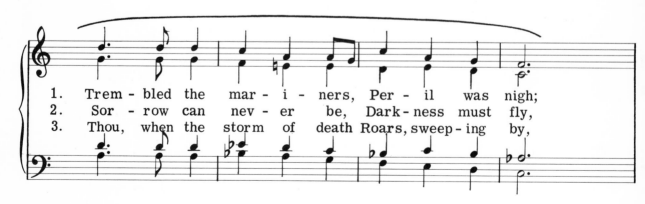

1. Trem - bled the mar - i - ners, Per - il was nigh;
2. Sor - row can nev - er be, Dark-ness must fly,
3. Thou, when the storm of death Roars, sweep-ing by,

1. Then said the God of God, 'Peace! it is I.'
2. Where saith the Light of light, 'Peace! it is I.'
3. Whis-per, O Truth of truth, 'Peace! it is I.'

FIRMLY I BELIEVE AND TRULY 11

J. Henry Newman, 1801–90

Henry Bryan Hays
CREDO 8.7. 8.7.

Firmly, stately

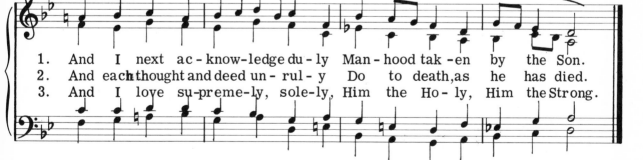

1. Firm-ly I be-lieve and tru-ly God is Three, and God is One;
2. And I trust and hope most ful-ly In that Man-hood cru-ci-fied;
3. Simp-ly to his grace and whol-ly Light and life and strength be-long,

1. And I next ac-know-ledge du-ly Man-hood tak-en by the Son.
2. And each thought and deed un-rul-y Do to death, as he has died.
3. And I love su-preme-ly, sole-ly, Him the Ho-ly, Him the Strong.

4. And I hold in veneration,
   For the love of him alone,
   Holy Church as his creation,
   And her teachings as his own.

5. Adoration ay be given,
   With and through th' angelic host,
   To the God of earth and heaven,
   Father, Son, and Holy Ghost.

12   FLOWER OF WISDOM

(Based on Sirach, Ch. 1)
Benedict Neale Lundgren, OSB, b. 1951
alt.

Henry Bryan Hays
GLORY BAND IRREG.

With easy movement

1. I stand in ho - ly fear
2. A shore whose sands re - veal

Be - fore the Glo - ry
The bed of a time-worn

1. Band,
2. sea—

En - rap - tured by the ly - ric strand now
A rain - es-tranged, e - ter - nal spring still

1. weav - ing
2. sound - ing—

A coat that I would wear,
Is a des - ert I have ren-dered,

A
A

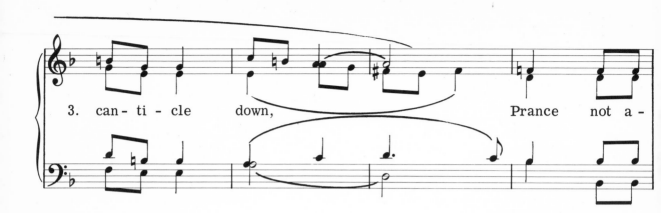

3. can - ti - cle   down,   Prance   not a-

3. cross the hal - lowed hall   Lest you dark - en the light,   Throw a

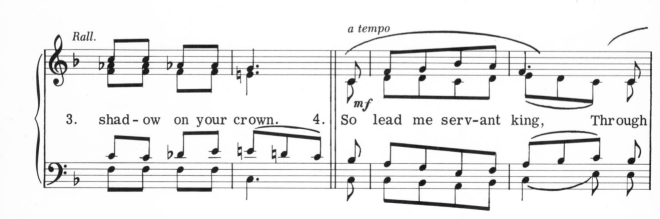

3. shad - ow on your crown.   4. So   lead me serv-ant king,   Through

13   FOREVER AND ALWAYS HE TRULY IS GOD

(Phil. 2:6-11)

Bro. Louis Blenkner, OSB, b. 1922

Henry Bryan Hays
FORT DONELSON 11.9. 11.7

Somewhat slowly

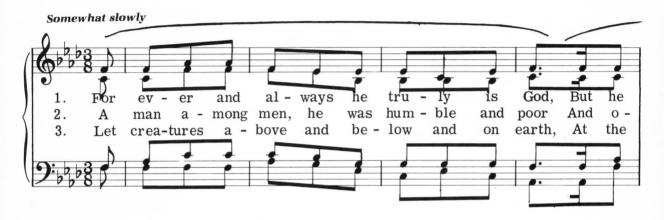

1. For ev - er and al - ways he tru - ly is God, But he
2. A man a - mong men, he was hum - ble and poor And o -
3. Let crea-tures a - bove and be - low and on earth, At the

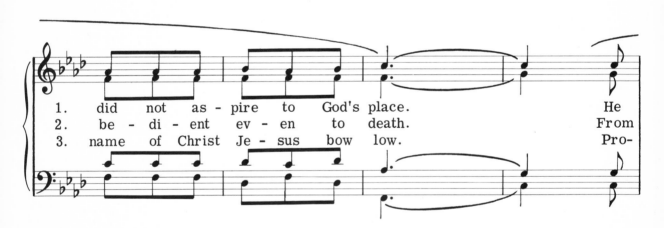

1. did not as - pire to God's place.   He
2. be - di - ent ev - en to death.   From
3. name of Christ Je - sus bow low.   Pro-

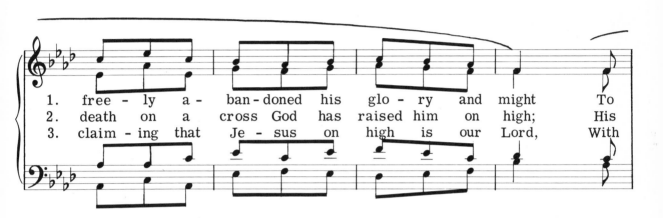

1. free - ly a - ban-doned his glo - ry and might To
2. death on a cross God has raised him on high; His
3. claim - ing that Je - sus on high is our Lord, With

1. serve and to walk with men.
2. name is a - bove the rest.
3. praise to our Fa - ther, God.

14   GOD MOVES IN A MYSTERIOUS WAY

William Cowper, 1731–1800

Henry Bryan Hays
RAPPAHANNOCK C.M.D.

Moderato tranquillo ♩ = 100

1. God moves in a mys- te - rious way His won-ders to per-
2. cour - age take; The clouds ye so much
3. rip - en fast, Un - fold - ing ev' - ry

1. form;   He plants his foot-steps in the sea, And
2. dread   Are big with mer - cy, and shall break In
3. hour;   The bud may have a bit - ter taste, But

1. rides up on the storm. Deep in un - fath - om -
2. bless - ings on your head. Judge not the Lord by
3. sweet will be the flower. Blind un - be - lief is

1. a - ble mines Of nev - er - fail - ing skill, He
2. fee - ble sense, But trust him for his grace; Be -
3. sure to err, And scan his work in vain; God

1. treas - ures up his bright de - signs, And works his sov - reign
2. hind a frown - ing Prov - i - dence He hides a smil - ing
3. is his own in - ter - pre - ter, And he will make it

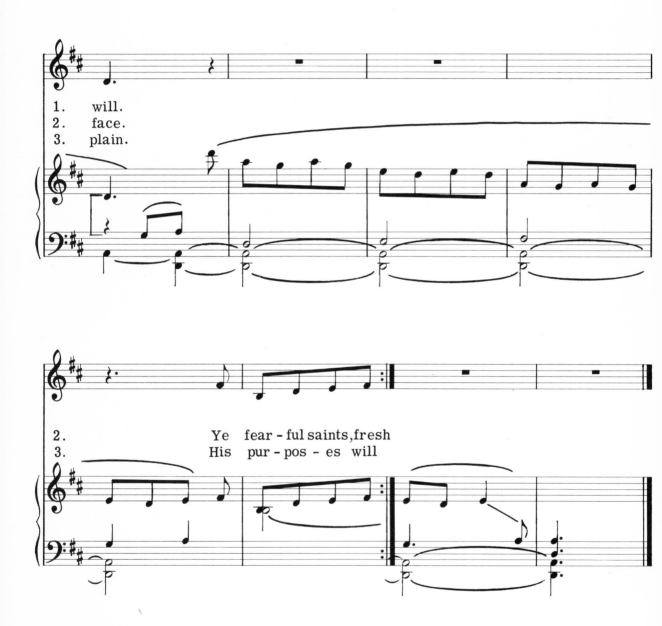

1. will.
2. face.
3. plain.

2.
3.

Ye fear - ful saints, fresh
His pur - pos - es will

GOD UNSEEN IS SEEN IN CHRIST

(Col. 1:15-20)

15

Bro. Louis Blenkner, osb, b. 1922

Henry Bryan Hays
INDIAN MOUND 7.8. 7.8.

Moderate time

1. God un - seen is seen in Christ, First - born son a-
2. Through him, for him, God has made Thrones, Do - min - ions,
3. Christ gives life to all that live, Christ is head, the

1. bove all crea - tures. God cre - a - ted all through him,
2. Princ es, Pow - ers. He was first be - fore all things;
3. Church his bod - y. First - born of the dead he reigns

1. Seen and un - seen, earth and heav - en.
2. In him all things hold to - geth - er.
3. First be - fore all God's cre - a - tion.

4 God has chosen that the Son,
   Fully God in his own nature,
   Buy with blood shed on the Cross
   Peace and reconciliation.

16 I LIFT MINE EYES UNTO THE HILLS

(Ps. 120)

Henry Bryan Hays

Henry Bryan Hays
ROSSVIEW C.M.

1. I lift mine eyes un to the hills; From
2. He'll suf – fer not your feet to fall, Nor
3. At your right hand he stands to give Pro-

1. where shall come my help? My help is from the
2. fail your path to keep. Be – hold, he that guards
3. tec – tion with his might. The sun shall smite you

1. Lord who made The heav – ens, earth, and sea.
2. Is – ra – el Will slum – ber not nor sleep.
3. not by day, Nor shall the moon by night.

4. The Lord will guard you from all ill,
   Will keep your soul from sin.
   The Lord will keep your going out,
   Protect your coming in.

JESU, THOU JOY OF LOVING HEARTS

17

Ascribed to St. Bernard of Clairvaux, 1091–1155
Tr. Ray Palmer, 1808–87
(Slightly altered)

Henry Bryan Hays
(Suggested by a troubadour
melody of Bernart de Ventadorn,
12th c. French)
HARPERS FERRY L.M.D.

Flowing   ♩. = 48

1. Je - su, thou joy of lov - ing hearts, Thou
2. We taste thee, O thou liv - ing Bread, And
3. O Je - su, ev - er with us stay; Make

1. Fount of life, thou Light of men,
2. long to feast up - on thee still; We
3. all our mo - ments calm and bright;

Copyright © 1981 The Order of St. Benedict, Inc.

1. From the best bliss that earth im-parts We
2. drink of thee, the Foun - tain - head, And
3. Chase the dark night of sin a - way, Shed

1. turn un - filled to thee a - gain. Thy
2. thirst our souls from thee to fill. Our
3. o'er the world thy ho - ly light.

1. truth un-changed hath ev - er stood; Thou
2. rest - less spir - its yearn for thee, Where

1. sav - est those that on thee call; To
2. e'er our change - ful lot is cast; Glad,

1. them that seek thee thou art good, To
2. when thy gra - cious smile we see, Blest,

1. them that find thee, all in all.
2. when our faith can hold thee fast.

18 LET US, WITH A GLADSOME MIND

(Ps. 136)

John Milton, 1608–74

Henry Bryan Hays
HOPEWELL GAP
77. 7.7. 7.7. 7.7. D.

With movement

1. Let us, with a glad - some mind, Praise the Lord, for
2. He, with all - com - mand - ing might, Filled the new - made
3. He hath with a pit - eous eye, Looked up - on our

sustained

1. he is kind:
2. world with light: For his mer - cies aye en - dure,
3. mis - er - y:

19 LORD, TEACH US HOW TO PRAY ARIGHT

J. Montgomery, 1771–1854

Henry Bryan Hays
ELKHORN TAVERN 8.6.8.6. D.

With movement

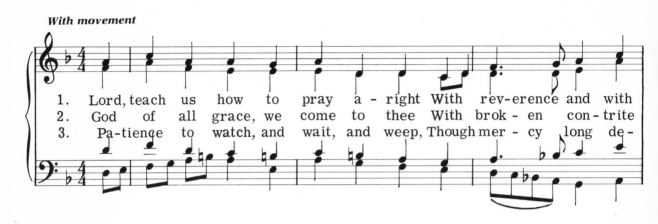

1. Lord, teach us how to pray a-right With rev-erence and with
2. God of all grace, we come to thee With brok-en con-trite
3. Pa-tience to watch, and wait, and weep, Though mer-cy long de-

1. fear; Though dust and ash-es in thy sight, We
2. hearts; Give, what thine eye de lights to see, Truth
3. lay; Cour-age our faint-ing souls to keep, And

1. may, we must draw near.   We per - ish if we
2. in the in - ward parts;   Faith in the on - ly
3. trust thee though thou slay.   Give these, and then thy

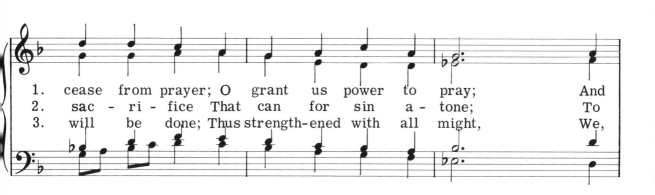

1. cease from prayer; O grant us power to pray;   And
2. sac - ri - fice That can for sin a - tone;   To
3. will be done; Thus strength-ened with all might,   We,

1. when to meet thee we pre-pare, Lord, meet us by the way.
2. cast our hopes, to fix our eyes, On Christ, on Christ a - lone;
3. through thy Spir- it and thy Son, Shall pray, and pray a - right.

20   LOVING SHEPHERD OF THY SHEEP

Jane E. Lesson, 1807–82

Henry Bryan Hays
PEA RIDGE 7.7. 7.7. D.

1. Lov - ing shep-herd of thy sheep,   Keep thy lamb, in safe-ty keep;
2. I would bless thee ev'-ry day,   Glad-ly all thy will o-bey,

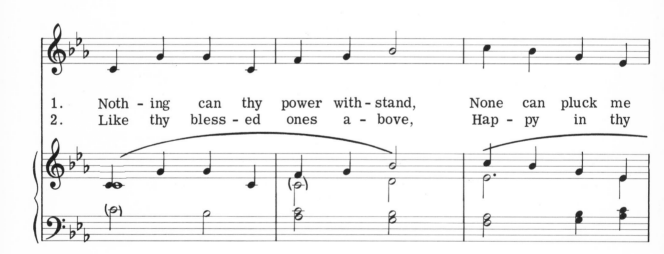

1. Noth - ing can thy power with-stand,   None can pluck me
2. Like thy bless-ed ones a-bove,   Hap-py in thy

1. from thy hand.
2. pre - cious love.

1. Lov - ing Sav - iour, thou didst give
2. Lov - ing Shep - herd, ev - er near,
3. Where thou lead I would go,

f

1. Thine own life that we might live; And the hands out -
2. Teach thy lamb thy voice to hear; Suf - fer not my
3. Walk - ing in thy steps be low, Till be - fore my

1. stretched to bless Bear the cru - el nails' im - press.
2. steps to stray From the straight and nar - row way.
3. Fa ther's throne I shall know as I am known.

21 O BLEST CREATOR OF THE LIGHT

(Lucis Creator optime)

6th cent.
Tr. J. M. Neale

Henry Bryan Hays
RADIANT LIGHT 8.8.8.8.D.

Moderately

1. O blest Cre-a-tor of the light, Who mak'st the day with ra-diance bright, And o'er the form-ing world didst call The light from cha-os first of all;

2. Whose wis-dom joined in meet ar-ray The morn and eve, and named them Day: Night comes with all its dark-ling fears; Re-gard thy peo-ple's prayers and tears,

3. Lest, sunk in sin, and whelm'd with strife, They lose the gift of end-less life; While think-ing but the thoughts of time, They weave new chains of woe and crime.

4. But grant them grace that they may strain
The heavenly gate and prize to gain:
Each harmful lure aside to cast,
And purge away each error past.

5. O Father, that we ask be done,
Through Jesus Christ, thine only Son;
Who, with the Holy Ghost and thee,
Doth live and reign eternally.

O CHRIST, WHO ART THE LIGHT AND DAY

(Christe qui lux es et dies)

Before 800
Tr. W. J. Copeland and others

Henry Bryan Hays

SHILOH L.M.D.

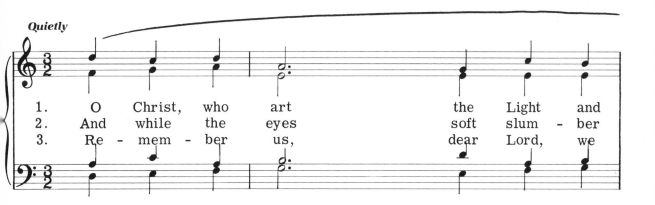

1. O Christ, who art the Light and
2. And while the eyes soft slum - ber
3. Re - mem - ber us, dear Lord, we

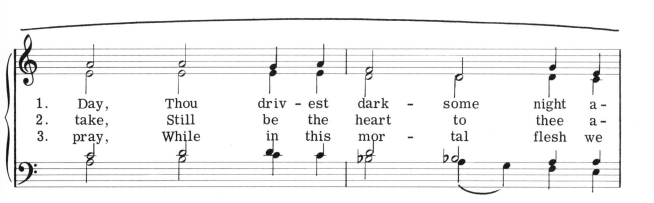

1. Day, Thou driv - est dark - some night a -
2. take, Still be the heart to thee a -
3. pray, While in this mor - tal flesh we

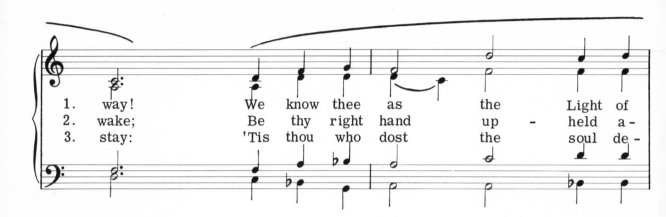

1. way!   We know thee as   the   Light of
2. wake;   Be thy right hand   up – held a-
3. stay: 'Tis thou who dost   the   soul de-

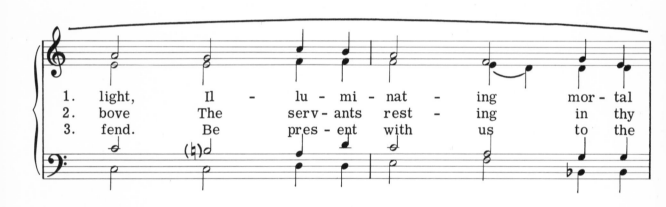

1. light,   Il –   lu – mi – nat – ing   mor – tal
2. bove   The   serv – ants rest – ing   in thy
3. fend.   Be   pres – ent with us   to the

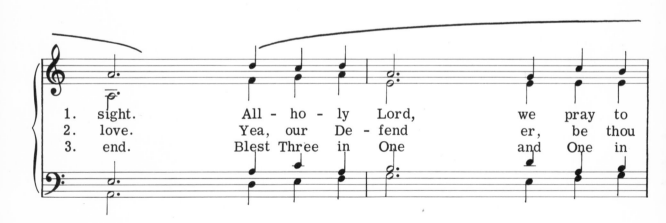

1. sight.   All – ho – ly Lord,   we pray to
2. love.   Yea, our De – fend   er, be thou
3. end.   Blest Three in One   and One in

1. thee, Keep us to-night from dan - ger
2. nigh To bid the powers of dark-ness
3. Three, Al – might - y God, we pray to

1. free; Grant us, dear Lord, in thee to
2. fly; Keep us from sin, and guide for
3. thee That thou wouldst now vouch – safe to

1. rest, So be our sleep in qui - et blest.
2. good Thy serv-ants pur - chased by thy Blood.
3. bless Our fast with fruits of right-eous-ness.

23   O FOR A CLOSER WALK WITH GOD

William Cowper, 1731–1800

Henry Bryan Hays
MANASSAS C.M.D.

With movement

1. O for a clos - er walk with God, A calm and heaven-ly
2. What peace - ful hours I once en - joyed! How sweet their mem-ory
3. The dear - est i - dol I have known, What-e'er that i - dol

1. frame, A light to shine up - on the road That
2. still! But they have left an ach - ing void The
3. be, Help me to tear it from thy throne, And

1. leads me to the Lamb. Where is the bless - ed-
2. world can nev - er fill. Re - turn, O ho - ly
3. wor - ship on - ly thee. So shall my walk be

1. ness I knew When first I saw the Lord? Where
2. Dove, re turn, Sweet mess - en - ger of rest! I
3. close with God, Calm and se - rene my frame; So

1. is the soul - re - fresh - ing view Of Je - sus and his
2. hate the sins that made thee mourn, And drove thee from my
3. pur - er light shall mark the road That leads me to the

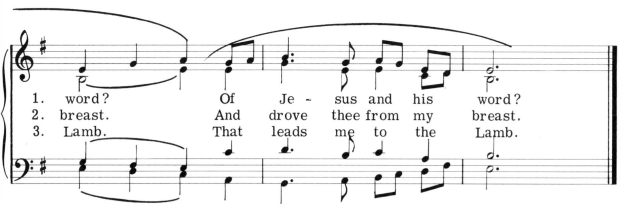

1. word? Of Je - sus and his word?
2. breast. And drove thee from my breast.
3. Lamb. That leads me to the Lamb.

24   O FOR A HEART TO PRAISE MY GOD

Charles Wesley, 1707–88

Henry Bryan Hays
DUNKER CHURCH C.M.D.

With movement

1. O for a heart to praise my God, A heart from sin set
2. A hum-ble, low-ly, con-trite heart, Be-liev-ing, true, and
3. My heart, thou know'st, can nev-er rest Till thou cre-ate my

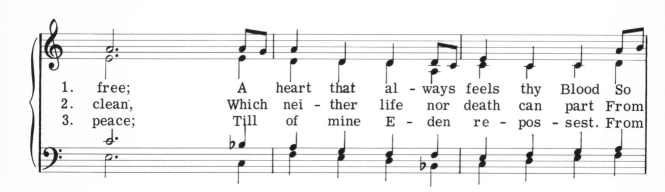

1. free; A heart that al-ways feels thy Blood So
2. clean, Which nei-ther life nor death can part From
3. peace; Till of mine E-den re-pos-sest. From

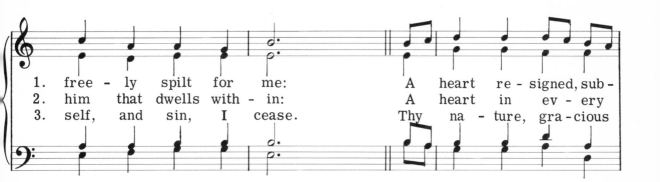

1. free - ly spilt for me: A heart re - signed, sub-
2. him that dwells with - in: A heart in ev - ery
3. self, and sin, I cease. Thy na - ture, gra - cious

1. miss - ive, meek My dear Re - deem - er's throne; Where
2. thought re - newed, And full of love di - vine; Per -
3. Lord, im - part, Come quick - ly from a - bove; Write

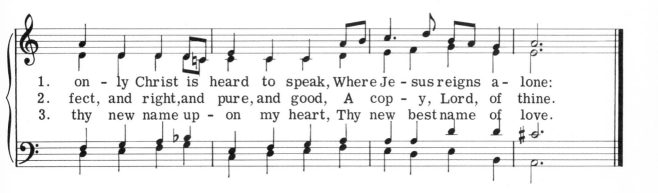

1. on - ly Christ is heard to speak, Where Je - sus reigns a - lone:
2. fect, and right, and pure, and good, A cop - y, Lord, of thine.
3. thy new name up - on my heart, Thy new best name of love.

25 O GOD, CREATION'S SECRET FORCE

Rerum Deus tenax vigor
Ascribed to St. Ambrose, 340–97
Tr. J. M. Neale

Henry Bryan Hays
CHICKAHOMINY 8. 8. 8. 8.

Moderate time

1. O God Cre - a - tion's se - cret force,
2. Grant us, when this short life is past
3. O Fa - ther, that we ask be done,

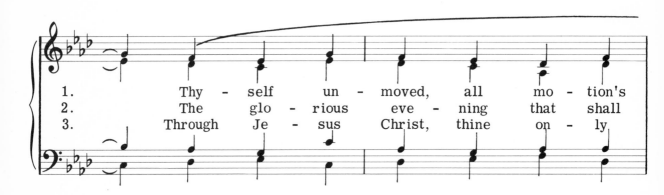

1. Thy - self un - moved, all mo - tion's
2. The glo - rious eve - ning that shall
3. Through Je - sus Christ, thine on - ly

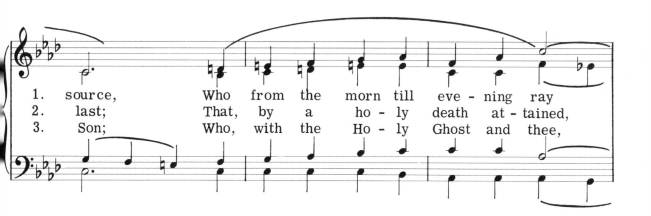

1. source, Who from the morn till eve - ning ray
2. last; That, by a ho - ly death at - tained,
3. Son; Who, with the Ho - ly Ghost and thee,

1. Through all its chang - es guid'st the day:
2. E - ter - nal glo - ry may be gained.
3. Doth live and reign e - ter - nal ly.

26 O LORD, MY PORTION AND MY CUP

Ps. 16
Henry Bryan Hays

Henry Bryan Hays
NEW HOPE CHURCH 8.6. 8.6. 8.6.

Smoothly

1. O Lord, my por - tion and my cup, 'Tis
2. By day the Lord gives me ad -vice, He
3. I set you, Lord, be - fore my eyes: My

1. you who are my prize. A
2. rules my wak - ing hours. By
3. gaze is fixed on you. On

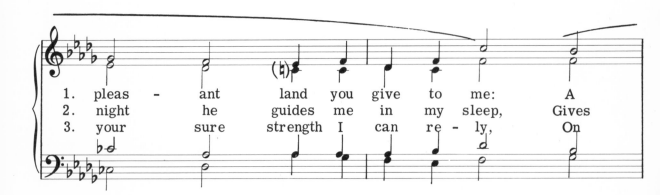

1. pleas - ant land you give to me: A
2. night he guides me in my sleep, Gives
3. your sure strength I can re - ly, On

1. good - ly her - i - tage. This
2. coun - sel to my heart. I
3. your help I can call. Be -

1. lot di - vine Is ev - er mine: My
2. bless the Lord Who by his word True
3. cause you stand At my right hand, I

1. treas - ure and my crown.
2. knowl - edge thus im - parts.
3. know I shall not fall.

4. And so my heart is ever glad;
   My spirit, full of joy.
   My body also rests in hope
   That it see not decay.
   For you will save
   Me from the grave:
   My soul you'll not destroy.

5. You'll show me, Lord, the path of life,
   That I may walk aright.
   A new heart, from which joy pours forth,
   Is work that you have wrought.
   In your right hand
   Are pleasures found
   Beyond the realm of thought.

O LOVE, HOW DEEP

15th cent.
Tr. B. Webb

Henry Bryan Hays
HAMPTON STATION L.M.

Sturdy

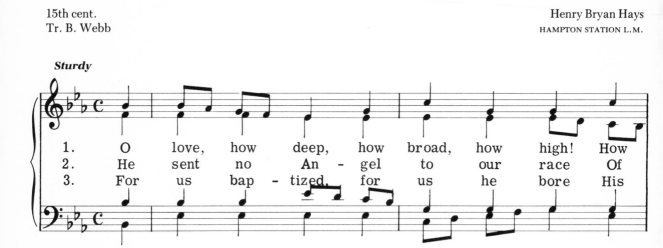

1. O love, how deep, how broad, how high! How
2. He sent no An - gel to our race Of
3. For us bap - tized, for us he bore His

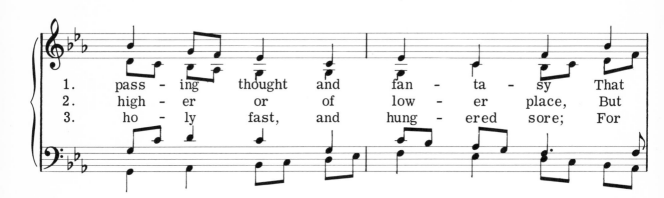

1. pass - ing thought and fan - ta - sy That
2. high - er or of low - er place, But
3. ho - ly fast, and hung - ered sore; For

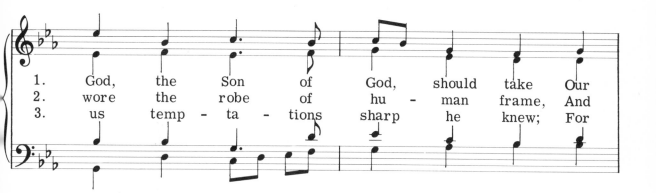

1. God, the Son of God, should take Our
2. wore the robe of hu - man frame, And
3. us temp - ta - tions sharp he knew; For

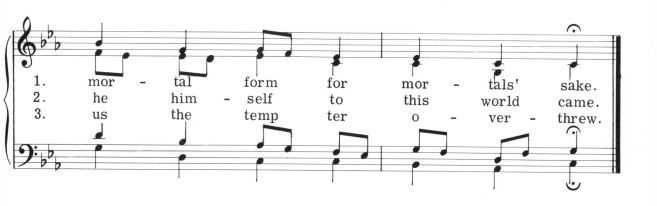

1. mor - tal form for mor - tals' sake.
2. he him - self to this world came.
3. us the temp ter o - ver - threw.

4. For us to wicked men betrayed,
   Scourged, mocked, in crown of thorns arrayed;
   For us he bore the Cross's death;
   For us at length gave up his breath.

5. For us he rose from death again,
   For us he went on high to reign,
   For us he sent his Spirit here
   To guide, to strengthen, and to cheer.

6. All honour, laud, and glory be,
   O Jesu, Virgin-born, to thee,
   All glory as is ever meet,
   To Father, and to Paraclete.

28   O WOULD I WERE A SNOW WHITE DOVE

Henry Bryan Hays

Henry Bryan Hays
MECHANICSVILLE 8.7. 8.7. D.

Freely, with intensity

1. O were I but a snow white dove, On
2. My soul is like that snow-y dove, On
3. Come, all you souls, be fear-ful not, On

1. high I would be soar-ing; Out to the de-sert I would
2. wings it would be ris-ing; Far from all e-vil it would
3. high, our wings un-fold-ing; Out to the de-sert let us

1. fly, Far from the storm clouds roar-ing. Un-
2. fly, Un-god-ly things de-spis-ing. Un-
3. fly, All e-vil things ab-hor-ing. Un-

1. to a moun-tain high I'd fly, To seek a peace-ful
2. to that moun-tain which is Christ, 'Twould fly to seek a
3. to that moun-tain which is Christ, Let's fly to seek a

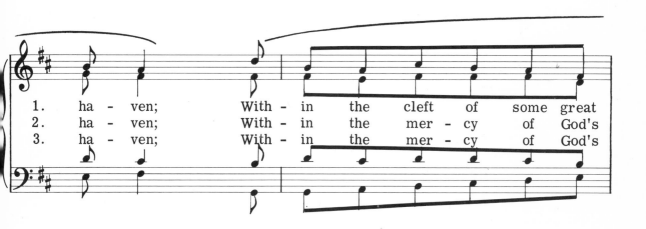

1. ha - ven; With - in the cleft of some great
2. ha - ven; With - in the mer - cy of God's
3. ha - ven; With - in the mer - cy of God's

1. rock, A re - fuge would be giv - en.
2. love, sure re - fuge I'd be giv - en.
3. love, We'll find the bliss of heav - en.

29 ONE THERE IS ABOVE ALL OTHERS

John Newton, 1725–1801

Henry Bryan Hays
FRIEND JESUS 8.7. 8.7. 7.7.

1. One there is a-bove all oth-ers, Well de-serves the
2. Which of all our friends, to save us, Could or would have
3. When he lived on earth a-bas-ed, 'Friend of sin-ners'

1. name of Friend; His is love be-yond a broth-er's
2. shed his blood? But this Sav-iour died to have us
3. was his Name; Now, a-bove all glo-ry rais-ed,

1. Cost - ly, free and knows no end; They who once his
2. Rec - on - ciled in him to God; This was bound-less
3. He re - joic - es in the same; Still he calls them

1. kind - ness prove Find it ev - er - last - ing love.
2. love in - deed; Je - sus is a friend in need.
3. breth - ren, friends, And to all their wants at tends.

4. O for grace our hearts to soften!
   Teach us, Lord, at length to love.
   We, alas, forget too often
   What a friend we have above;
   But when home our souls are brought
   We will love thee as we ought.

30   OUR LORD IS GOD WHO LIVES

Bro. Louis Blenkner, OSB, b. 1922

Henry Bryan Hays
PLUM RUN BEND 6.8. 7.7. 6.6.

With movement

1. Our Lord is God who lives, The
2. His pow – er made the earth, His
3. His thun – der shapes the storm, He

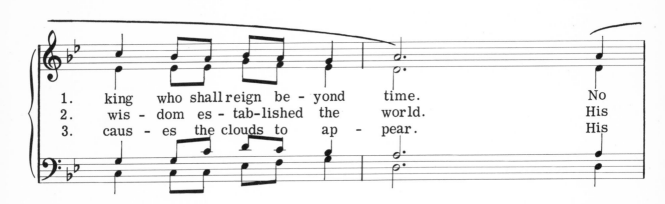

1. king who shall reign be - yond time. No
2. wis - dom es - tab-lished the world. His
3. caus - es the clouds to ap - pear. His

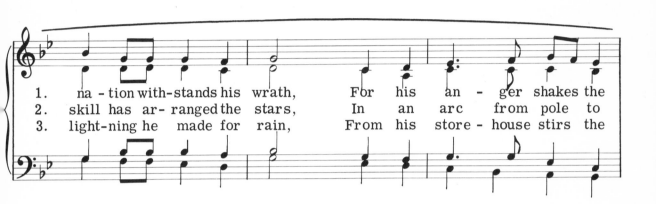

1. na - tion with-stands his wrath, For his an - ger shakes the
2. skill has ar- ranged the stars, In an arc from pole to
3. light-ning he made for rain, From his store - house stirs the

1. earth. Tru-ly the Lord is God! Tru-ly the Lord is God!
2. pole. Tru-ly the Lord is God! Tru-ly the Lord is God!
3. wind. Tru-ly the Lord is God! Tru-ly the Lord is God!

31 PRAISE THE LORD OF HEAVEN

Ps. 148
Thomas Brierly Browne, 1805–74

Henry Bryan Hays
HANOVER JUNCTION 6.5. 6.5. D.

Joyfully ♩=120

1. Praise the Lord of heav - en; Praise him in the height!
2. Praise the Lord of foun - tains Of the depths and seas;
3. Praise the Lord of na - tions, Ru - lers and all kings;

1. Praise him all ye an - gles; Praise him, stars and light;
2. Rocks and hills and moun - tains, Ce - dars and all trees;
3. Praise him, men and maid - ens, All cre - a ted things;

1. Praise him, earth and wa - ters, Praise him, all ye skies;
2. Praise him, clouds and va - pors, Snow and hail and fire,
3. Glo - ri - ous and might - y Is his name a - lone;

1. When his Word com-mand - ed, All things did a - rise.
2. Na - ture all ful - fill - ing On - ly his de - sire.
3. All the earth his foot - stool, Heav - en is his throne.

32

THE GOD OF LOVE MY SHEPHERD IS
(Ps. 23)

George Herbert, 1593–1632

Henry Bryan Hays

GLORIETA PASS C.M.D.

Quietly, but with movement

1. The God of love my Shep-herd is, And he that doth me
2. Or if I stray, he doth con-vert, And bring my mind in

1. feed; While he is mine and I am his, What
2. frame, And all this not for my de-sert, But

1. can I want or need?   He leads me to the
2. for his ho - ly name.   Yea, in death's shad - y
3.   Sure - ly thy sweet and

1. ten - der grass, Where I both feed and rest;   Then
2. black a - bode Well may I walk, not fear;   For
3. won - drous love Shall meas - ure all my days;   And

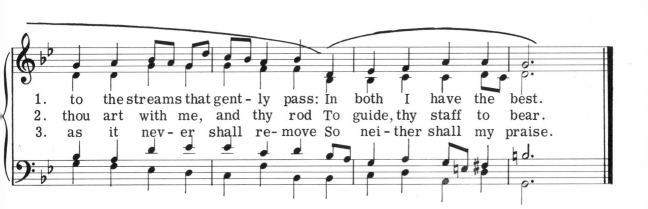

1. to the streams that gent - ly pass: In both I have the best.
2. thou art with me, and thy rod To guide, thy staff to bear.
3. as it nev - er shall re - move So nei - ther shall my praise.

33   THE KING OF LOVE MY SHEPHERD IS

Henry Williams Baker, 1821–77
Ps. 23

Henry Bryan Hays
ANTIETAM 8.7. 8.7.

Peacefully flowing   ♩ = 63

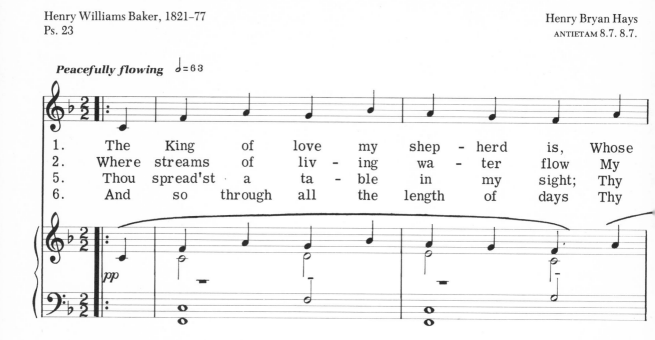

1. The King of love my shep - herd is, Whose
2. Where streams of liv - ing wa - ter flow My
5. Thou spread'st a ta - ble in my sight; Thy
6. And so through all the length of days Thy

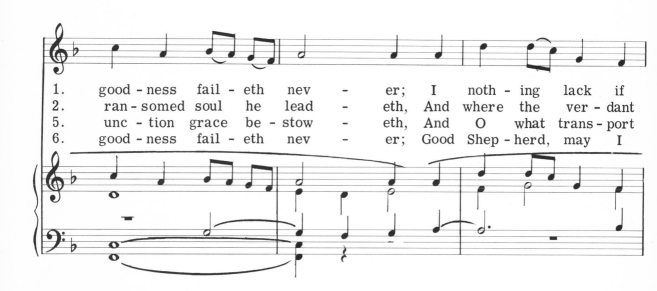

1. good - ness fail - eth nev - er; I noth - ing lack if
2. ran - somed soul he lead - eth, And where the ver - dant
5. unc - tion grace be - stow - eth, And O what trans - port
6. good - ness fail - eth nev - er; Good Shep - herd, may I

1. I am his, And he is mine for ev - er.
2. pas - tures grow With food ce - les - tial feed - eth.
5. and de - light From thy pure chal - ice flow - eth!
6. sing thy praise With in thy house for ev - er.

3. Per - verse and fool - ish oft I strayed, But
4. In death's dark vale I fear no ill With

3. yet in love he sought me And on his shoul - der
4. thee, dear Lord, be - side me Thy rod and staff my

3. gent - ly laid, And home, re - joic - ing brought me.
4. com - fort still, Thy Cross be - fore to guide me.

34A   THE LORD'S MY SHEPHERD

Scottish Psalter
Psalm 23

Henry Bryan Hays
CUMBERLAND GAP C.M.

Unison

1. The Lord's my shep - herd, I'll not want. He makes me

(Melody is the same as version 34A)

34B

THE LORD'S MY SHEPHERD

Scottish Psalter
Psalm 23

Henry Bryan Hays
CUMBERLAND GAP C.M.

Quietly

1. The Lord's my shep - herd, I'll not want. He makes me
2. My soul he doth re-store a - gain; and me to

pp

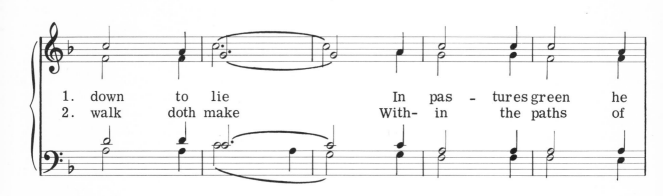

1. down to lie In pas - tures green he
2. walk doth make With- in the paths of

1. lead - eth me the qui - et wa - ters by,
2. right - eous-ness ev'n for his own name's sake,

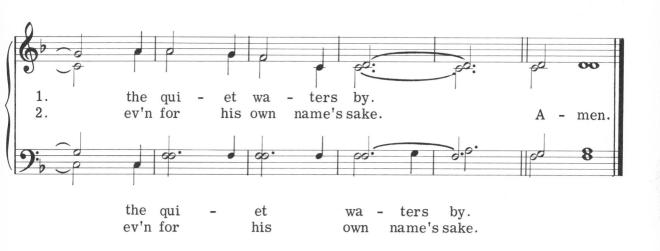

1. the qui - et wa - ters by.
2. ev'n for his own name's sake. A - men.

the qui - et wa - ters by.
ev'n for his own name's sake.

3. Yea, though I walk in death's dark vale,
    yet will I fear none ill:
  For thou art with me, and thy rod
    and staff me comfort still.

4. My table thou has furnished
    in presence of my foes;
  My head with oil thou dost anoint,
    and my cup overflows.

5. Goodness and mercy all my life
    shall surely follow me;
  And in God's house for evermore
    my dwelling place shall be.

35

THE LORD'S MY SHEPHERD

Henry Bryan Hays
Ps. 23

Henry Bryan Hays
SUNSHINE CHURCH 5.4. 5.4. D.

1. The Lord's my shep-herd; I shall not want.
2. Though I should walk in Death's dark-some vale,
3. He has pre-pared a Ban-quet for me

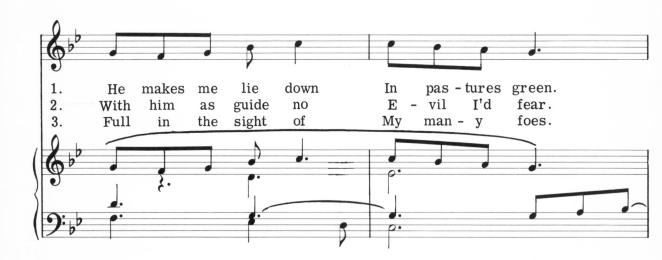

1. He makes me lie down In pas-tures green.
2. With him as guide no E - vil I'd fear.
3. Full in the sight of My man - y foes.

1. Near rest - ful streams Re - fresh - ment I find.
2. There with his crook And there with his staff:
3. He has a - noint - ed My head with oil.

1. True to his name, his Path's safe and sound.
2. These give me com - fort, New - ness of life.
3. Gen'-rous - ly filled, my cup o - ver - flows.

4. Surely his goodness
   Shall follow me;
   Likewise his kindness,
   Eternally.
   In the Lord's own house,
   All of my days,
   I'll sing forever
   Songs in his praise.

36

THE SONG OF THE TREES

Henry Bryan Hays
Ps. 96

Henry Bryan Hays
SAYLOR'S CREEK
9.7. 8.6. with Refrain

1. O sing to the Lord a song that's new, A
2. In deed he is worth - y to be praised; All
3. Let heav - en ex - ult and earth be glad, The

1. song for the Lord of all. Pro - claim his help each
2. glo - ry and might are his. An of - fering bring in it
3. sea thun - der forth its praise. Let earth and all it

1. day that comes, His won - drous works and deeds.
2. to his courts, His king - ship there pro - claim.
3. bears re - joice Be - fore the Lord who comes.

4. The presence of God is everywhere,
   He comes now to rule the earth.
   With justice he will govern all,
   All people judge with truth.

37 THOSE WHO TRUST IN THEMSELVES

(Jer. 17:5f.)

Bro. Louis Blenkner, OSB, b. 1922
(alt.)

Henry Bryan Hays
DESERT SHRUB 6.9. 6.7. 7.8.

With movement

1. Those who trust in them - selves And be -
2. But those who trust in God Are se -
3. The hu - man heart is sick And per -

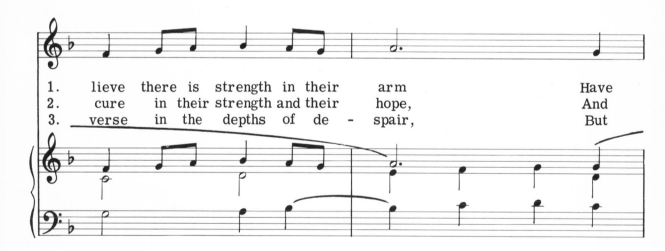

1. lieve there is strength in their arm Have
2. cure in their strength and their hope, And
3. verse in the depths of de - spair, But

1. turned their minds from God. They dwell on dry salt
2. dwell be - side a brook. They grow like strong green
3. who can know our hearts? God tests and search - es the

1. plains Like twist - ed des - ert shrubs And
2. trees, Send - ing roots through rich damp earth And
3. heart, And he gives to all of us Due

ped. 16' (actual sounds)

1. nev — er see good when it comes.
2. ev — en in dry years bear fruit.
3. wage for the fruit of our ways.

38 TO MERCY, PITY, PEACE AND LOVE

William Blake, 1757–1827

Henry Bryan Hays
EVELINGTON HEIGHTS C.M.D.

With movement

1. To Mer - cy, Pit - y, Peace and Love, all pray in their dis-
2. For Mer - cy has a hu - man heart, Pit - y a hu - man

1. tress; and to those vir - tues of de - light re-
2. face, and Love, the hu - man form di - vine, and

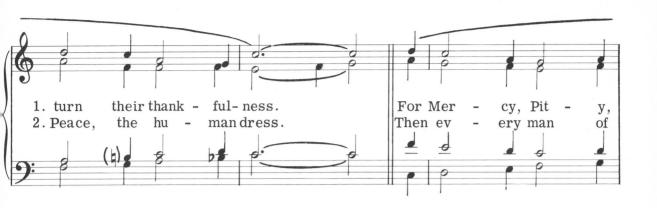

1. turn   their thank - ful- ness.   For Mer - cy, Pit - y,
2. Peace, the hu - man dress.   Then ev - ery man   of

1. Peace   and Love   is God   our fa - ther dear,   and
2. ev - ery clime   that prays   in his   dis-tress,   prays

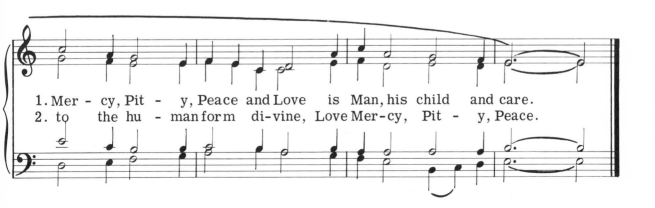

1. Mer - cy, Pit - y, Peace and Love   is Man, his child   and care.
2. to   the hu - man form di - vine, Love Mer-cy, Pit - y, Peace.

39 WE PRAISE YOU, GOD
(Te Deum)

Bro. Louis Blenkner, osb, b. 1922

Henry Bryan Hays
MONTANA 8.8.8. 7.8.

Brisk and lively

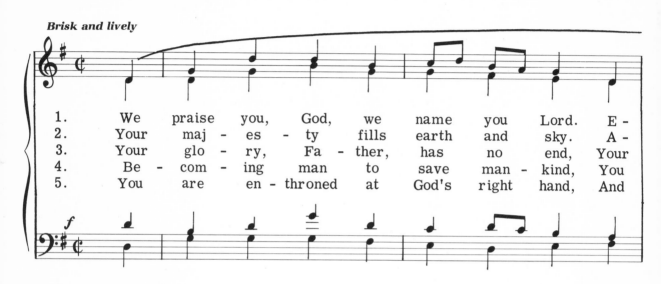

1. We praise you, God, we name you Lord. E-
2. Your maj - es - ty fills earth and sky. A-
3. Your glo - ry, Fa - ther, has no end, Your
4. Be - com - ing man to save man - kind, You
5. You are en - throned at God's right hand, And

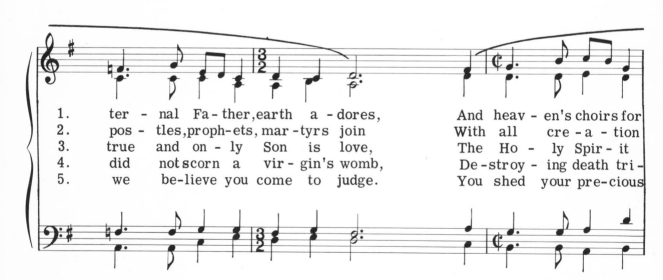

1. ter - nal Fa - ther, earth a - dores, And heav - en's choirs for
2. pos - tles, proph-ets, mar-tyrs join With all cre - a - tion
3. true and on - ly Son is love, The Ho - ly Spir - it
4. did not scorn a vir - gin's womb, De - stroy - ing death tri-
5. we be - lieve you come to judge. You shed your pre - cious

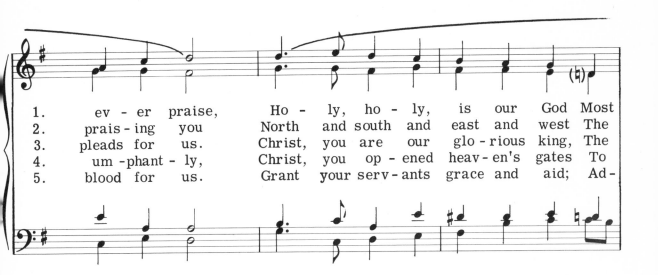

1. ev - er praise,   Ho - ly, ho - ly, is our God Most
2. prais - ing you   North and south and east and west The
3. pleads for us.   Christ, you are our glo - rious king, The
4. um -phant - ly,   Christ, you op - ened heav - en's gates To
5. blood for us.   Grant your serv - ants grace and aid; Ad-

1. ho - ly is the Lord   of all.
2. Church pro -claims her faith   in you.
3. Fa -ther's own e - ter   nal Son.
4. all be - liev - ers in   your word.
5. mit us all a - mong   your saints.

(See following pages for additional harmonization
and descant for choir)

Version with melody in the tenor for stanza four

4. Be - com - ing man to save man - kind, You

4. did not scorn a vir - gin's womb   De - stroy - ing death tri -

4. um - phant - ly,   Christ, you op - ened heav - en's gates   To

4. all be - liev - ers in   your word.

Descant for stanza five

5.   You   are   en - throned   at   God's   right

5.   hand,   And   we   be - lieve   you   come   to

5.   judge.   Ad - mit   us   all

5.   a - mong, a - mong   your   saints.

40 WHEN I SURVEY THE WONDROUS CROSS

Isaac Watts, 1674–1748

Henry Bryan Hays
CONRAD'S STORE L.M.

Stately (in Sarabande tempo) ♩ = 69

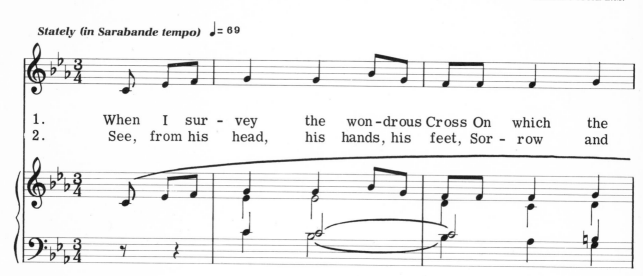

1. When I sur - vey the won-drous Cross On which the
2. See, from his head, his hands, his feet, Sor - row and

1. Prince of Glo - ry died, My rich-est gain I count but
2. love flow min-gled down; Did e'er such love and sor - row

1. loss   And pour con - tempt   on   all my   pride.   For - bid it,
2. meet,   Or thorns com - pose   so   rich a   crown?   Were the whole

1. Lord,   that   I should boast   Save   in the   death   of   Christ, my
2. realm   of   na - ture mine,   That were an   of - f'ring   far too

1. God;   All   the vain   things   that   charm me
2. small;   Love   so   a - maz   - ing,   so di-

1. most, I sac - ri - fice   them   to his   Blood.
2. vine, De - mands   my   soul,   my life, my   all.